Through My Father's Eyes
Words that brought us closer together

Patrick A. de Werk

Through My Father's Eyes, by Patrick A. de Werk

Copyright © 2020, 2023, Patrick A. de Werk

All rights reserved. No part of this publication may be reproduced, distributed, or transmitted in any form or by any means, including photocopying, recording, or other electronic or mechanical methods, without the prior written permission of the author, except in the case of brief quotations embodied in critical reviews.

Published by CdeW Artistry and Patrick de Werk

Printed in the United States of America

Back Cover Image by Capri23auto from Pixabay.

ISBN 978-1-7366265-4-2

Second Edition

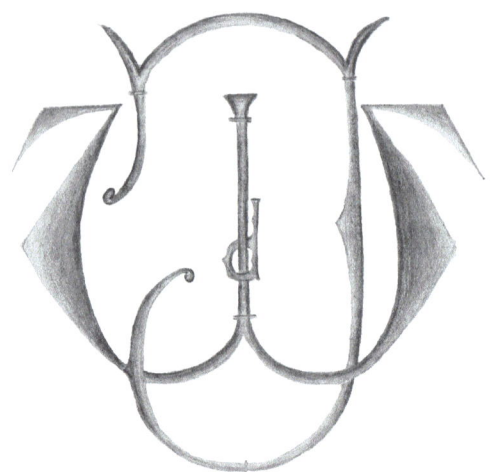

*This book is dedicated in memory of my Father
Jacobus "Jac" de Werk.
Who survived his childhood and many other adversities,
bringing his new family to a new world, starting a new life,
by leaving his other family and friends behind.
He was a great man, father, and hero!*

"I hope to be like you someday"

Trains

Now that my father is gone
I have his trains I grew up with
Never allowed to play with them
They now stand in silent display

Table of Contents

Trains ....
Through My Father's Eyes 1
Rotterdam 2
Life Was Hard 3
Emigrant 5
Visiting Anne 7
Piano Man 9
Dad 11
And They Danced 13
Christmas Splendor 15
Saying Goodbye 16
I'll Miss You 19
I will rest now 21
My Brother 21
Superman 23
A Prayer for a Morning Ride 25
My Father Wore Tails 27
My Little Girl 29
Visions 30
My Family 30
My Son 31
Cold Kiss Goodbye 33
I hope to be like you someday 35
Kind Words, Open Ears, Soft Shoulder, Shedding Tears 37
The Poet 39

Foreword

I was relaxing one afternoon in February of 2020, when my cell phone buzzed telling me that I had received a text. I checked my phone and found that the text was from Patrick de Werk, a very dear and close friend of over thirty years. He was writing to inform me that he had written a book of poetry and wanted to know if I would be willing to write the foreword. Patrick has numerous friends, any one of whom he could have asked, and any one of which would have said yes. I was honored at this request and gladly said yes.

Patrick and I became acquainted when I was a senior and he was a freshman in high school. We lived two houses away from each other on the same street and I would occasionally catch a ride to school with him and his brother. However, up until my graduation that was the entirety of our acquaintance. Then in the fall of 1983 he and I were members of the technical crew at a local production of Peter Pan, and we would ride to and from rehearsals and performances together. That is when this special relationship began.

Patrick and I both have artistic tendencies. His led him to poetry and mine led me to music. We have always supported each other in our artistic pursuits. As a music major in college, I took a class where I had to write, arrange, and perform songs for the class. I wrote a song called "Lots of Dough" and called on Patrick to assist with vocals. The song wasn't great but we had fun doing it, and I liked the finished product. Later when Patrick began writing poetry it was my turn to be supportive. I even participated in his poetry by supplying him with titles to work with, and then he would write the poem. The only ones I can recall are "Thunder Bay" and another entitled "Periwinkle and Puce".

Although I have read a majority of the poems Patrick has written, most of those in this collection are new to me. One in particular does stand out. It is the one he titled "Dad". This one is particularly poignant because the circumstances behind it. Patrick was driving one rainy day when he was involved in a serious automobile accident that totaled the family car. He wasn't badly injured and was able to walk away from it. Later, upon seeing the mangled condition of what had been the family station wagon, the implications of what the outcome could have been hit his father with full force. The next time they saw each other, his father, with great emotion, told his son how much he loved him. It was the first time that his father had spoken those words to him. And it was the first time he had ever seen his father cry.

Much of Patrick's poetry, just as my song lyrics, tends to be autobiographical! We both find inspiration in our personal experiences. As we approached the transition from our twenties into our thirties Patrick and I took a hiatus from artistic output as other particulars of life such as jobs and relationships took precedence. Work mostly took Patrick from his writing as he was obliged to travel the world, as was required by his job, which is how he met Kathy, the love of his life. Weary of that, he found another job where he could be home every evening. They would live in Utah and then Massachusetts. We didn't see each other for several years until they came home to California.

Poetry would remain on the back burner as his role as husband and father became his priority. Finally, as his daughter became a teenager and required a lesser amount of his time, he was able to once again put pen to paper and begin churning out the poetry that, though long dormant, was still inside him. I am proud of my friend. I respect and appreciate his talent. My hope is that this collection will not be the last his literary efforts. I know from personal experience, artistic expression can be and is quite therapeutic, and I am grateful to be permitted to contribute to this work. One of the things created by man that lasts and has a lasting impact is the written word. Long after Patrick and I have passed from this life, this book will remain. Enjoy.

~Leonard P. Adams

Preface

My father and I were not close when I was a child. But he was very much a family man.

He took photographs and movies, which he proudly put in albums and showed on movie nights. This showed how proud he was of us.

Occasionally we could help him with projects around the house, especially when it required crawling in tight spaces. His trusting us to do something was his way of showing he cared.

My father was kind and loving, but in little ways, like tucking us in bed at night. He watched over us in silence.

He didn't speak about his childhood much, only about things like his band, piano, and other surface things.

He liked camping with the family, but he always stayed at camp relaxing with the dog while we went hiking or something. He did try and teach me how to fish, even though he really didn't know how himself.

As I grew older, he embraced that I wrote. He came to poetry readings, and we were able to talk more when I wrote pieces about imagery of his life, that I could gather from what little he spoke about. In turn he would discuss with me further those images as I described, so I started to understand him more. Such as his childhood growing up during World War II in Rotterdam, the Netherlands. Which explained why I was never allowed to watch war movies in the house when he was around!

As we grew closer, we started riding motorcycles, going to the range, participating in organizational groups, and spending more time together, socializing and sometimes having in depth meaningful conversations.

He really opened up when my daughter was born. That's when we started to have a close relationship.

In his honor, the amazing relationship I had with him, and because of my writing, our motorcycle enthusiasm, and the deep love he had for my daughter Caitlin, I put together several poems he was proud of, made him (us) cry, and brought joy to his heart.

Acknowledgments

Maria T. (Maritha) de Werk-Mann. For spending time digging up photographs. The engraved plaque in memory of my father. The tireless nights at the hospital and at home. Thank you Mama!

Kathleen R. (Kathy) de Werk. Putting up with my hours of disappearing to prepare this book. For being the best wife and partner, supporting me and my parents, through everything. Your idea to have them move closer to us gave me the opportunity to be there when my father needed me most.

Caitlin E. de Werk. An inspirational young woman that brought out the best in my father and me together. You could always get your Opa to smile, laugh and do crazy things!

Craig F. (C.J.) Vickery. Responsible for getting me into public reading. Giving me inspiration and confidence. Without your push, this book may never have happened. Always my best man and best friend.

Leonard P. Adams. The one person who has read nearly everything I've ever written. Giving me inspiration to continue writing, providing subject matter, titles and other material. Another exceptionally close and amazing best friend.

Carissa K. Harrild. My closest and dearest friend (my work wife). Your understanding helped me get through everything. Supporting me after your father's passing couldn't be easy. We laughed and cried together (a lot). Thank you for inspiring another poem (found within these pages). Where would I be without you?

Vanessa L. A. Armstrong. My work cohort and amazing friend. Your constant support at work, talking, texting and IM, kept me going through bad days. You kept me smiling and laughing when I needed it, and listened when I needed to vent. "I Like Skittles!"

Katelyn E. (Katie) Smith. Someone I will never stop calling my friend. Thank you for reaching out, showing you understood what I was going through. Walking and talking was uplifting, and a welcome change to the workday. Noticing when I was "in a mood" and always there with kind words and a warm smile.

Robin S. (Rob) Rackwitz. Helping with my father's rehabilitation gave him strength to push on. He didn't want to disappoint you.

I laughed and cried with all of you, and I love you all so much!

Through My Father's Eyes
Words that brought us closer together

Patrick A. de Werk

Through My Father's Eyes

I was 10 when the soldiers came
I was never afraid of the dark before then
When the lights went out I heard the rumble
Sometimes the blasts were close by
Other times far away
Always afraid our house would be next

When they marched through the street
Mother's would hold their children tight
Father's would shuffle their families inside
Sometimes there was screaming
Someone is being chased again
I always wonder what they had done

Friends and neighbors moved at night
Mother said it was easier that way
But she never said why this was so
I had learned what was happening
Mother was just trying to protect us
The less we knew the better, she said

Often I awoke to gunfire and then a scream
Other nights first the scream then the gunfire
School was also often difficult for some time
Children whispered but could not talk aloud
As friends, one by one, stopped coming to class
Instructors forbade any questions asked

Five long years we lived like this
It seemed it would never end
Some friends came to school with pistols
And being older the talk also changed
"Did you hear about Johan's Father?"
"He was taken last night, right out of bed."

It's all over now, for some that is
Over a half century later I still feel the scars
I can't see the films, can't talk about the life
My family was fortunate not to be labeled
We were not of the chosen class
There was a lot of death then, even in the survivors

Rotterdam

My country surrendered to Evil
With the promise of salvation
The apocalypse came anyway

Fire and stone the sky fell
The end of the world upon us
Our city crumbled around us

By a grace beyond the bombers
My family lived through catastrophe
Thousands of others gone in minutes

Our city all but flattened
A church and a hotel still stood
As did the people together

A dozen more bombings came
But all from the "good guys"
To eradicate the Evil within our broken walls

We rebuilt our city
We rebuilt our lives
But we live with the scars forever

Life Was Hard

Our adolescence taken
Guns in school underground
With soldiers on the roof

Tulip bulbs for dinner
When there was nothing else
Sawdust in the bread

Our candy taken for beer
Our friends for peace
Keep still or disappear

Five years of fear and hate
Family sent to workcamps
Others lost in hiding

In peace with those we loved
As life had to go on
Survival a daily ritual

Canadians came to save us
To the World's hotel
From a continent away

No more soldiers
No more fighting
No more fear

The years of my life lost
Will never leave my mind
Vivid yet hidden away

From all the death and fear
I learned kindness to everyone
Hate has no place in my heart

Emigrant

After the war we struggled
Many people left or went missing

My family did what we could
Though we were better off than many

Growing and starting my own family
I packed us all and left as well

Separated from my family and friends
We struggled again with little we had

Life gave us adversity but we overcame
Growing what little we had to comfort

Losing family abroad not saying goodbye
And very few we could visit before passing

Life was hard after the war
And just as hard in the U.S.

But we had opportunities here
We became strong, independent, and secure

ANNE
FRANK
HUIS

Visiting Anne

My father and I went for a visit
To the home of a girl whom he grew up with
He didn't know her when he was a child
But he knows her childhood
He lived in a neighboring town
Growing up with children like her

I also grew up with her
But I didn't know her like my father
So I went to learn of her life
Understand how my father grew up
Read the walls and see the rooms
Grasp a different consciousness

I learned more than I expected
Not only the horror of the holocaust
But the pain that lingers through generations
My father quickly left the house
He was reliving the suffering of millions
His visit brought back too much pain

I never realized how powerful a memory could be
How paralyzed a nation had become
How potent emotions could be aroused by mere words
By actually being in the place a little girl's diary described
Being in the halls where blood was spilled
Living the grief only from the presence of its remains

She no longer lives in the house
Nor is she alive to know her fame
But she lives on, as the house is there
And this sort of fame we can all live without
From being in her home I have lived her life
Knowing now why my father never shared his

ROTTERDAM
MATHENESSERWEG 57
TELEFOON 50271

The Sunrisers
o.l.v. Jac. de Werk

VOOR DANS, AMUSEMENT EN BRUILOFTEN

Piano Man

I played piano since I was six
Playing through war and strife
Through good times and bad
It made me happy when sad

I composed music for the radio
That big named bands would play
I wrote for friends and family
Some are still played to this day

I had my own band The Sunrisers
After 15 years I left behind
To bring my family overseas
For a better life I had planned

We started our own family band
Together we would play
And each night after dinner
I'd play the night away

The piano got me through my life
Through every passing day
I never gave the piano up
Because life was better that way

Dad

Lights flashed, sirens wailed
Traffic backed up like rush hour
As rubber-neckers eyed the wreckage
Rain soaked paramedics
Pull a limp lifeless body
From the twisted mass of metal
Family members rushed unknowingly to the hospital
Hoping against all hope
That their loved one would still have some sign of life
After seeing the remains
A once totally emotionless father
Gave way to a flood of tears
He wrapped his arms around his son who was awakening
And said "I love you" for the first time

And They Danced

To my graduation
Came my parents dear

They laughed and drank
Enjoyed themselves
And all the party cheer

They both got up
Onto the floor
And then began to dance

With sheer delight
My friends all watched
They danced just once that night

Are those your parents
Throughout they asked
Yes they belong to me

I figured they would cause me grief
Instead they made me happy

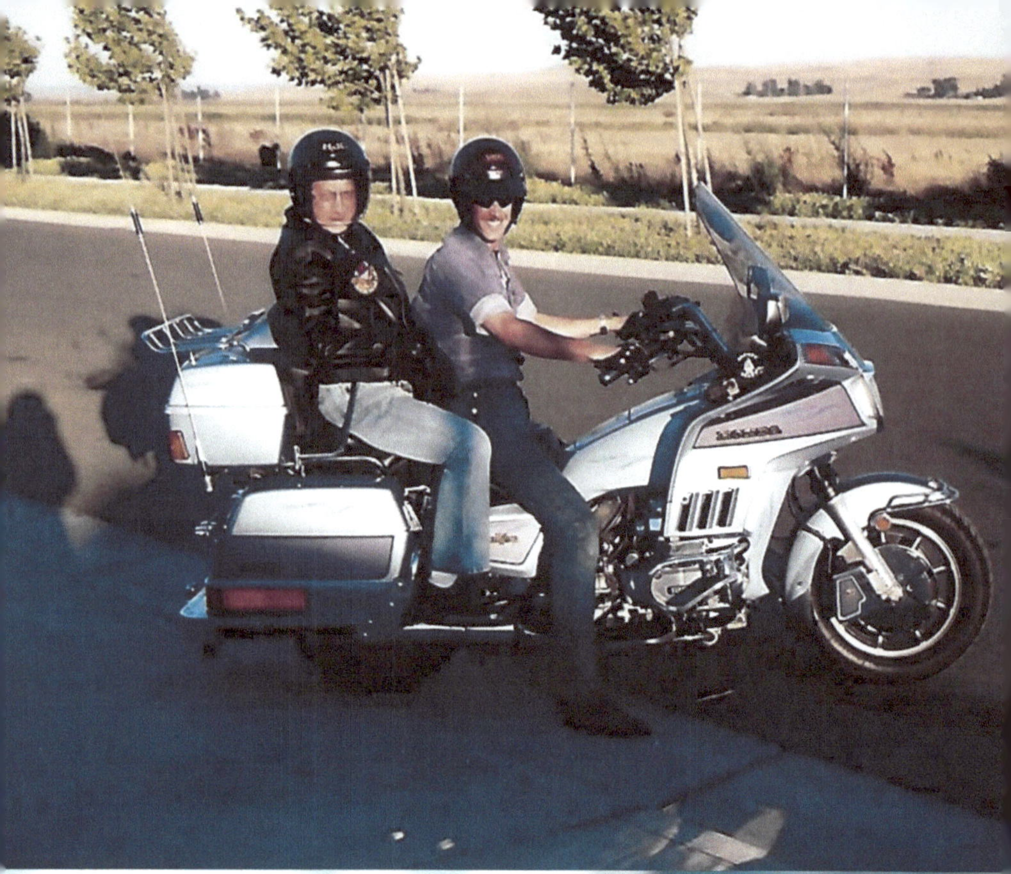

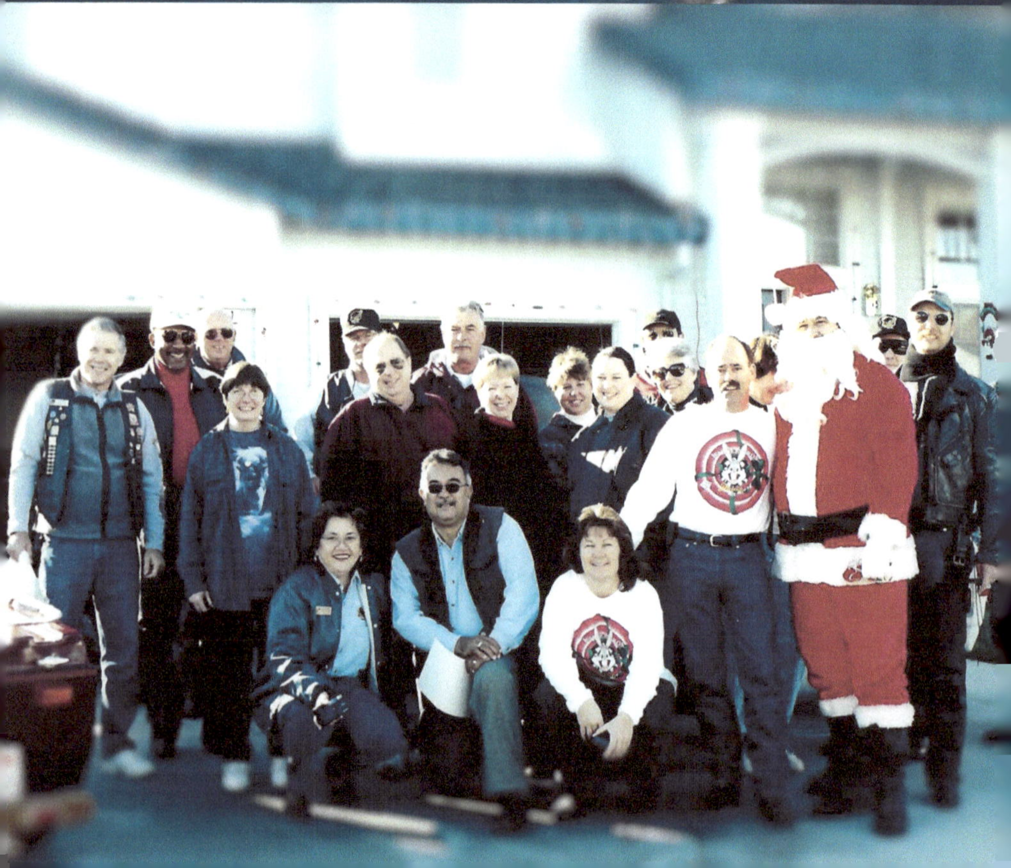

Christmas Splendor

We ride Gold Wings
How appropriate for today
We are angels
Lead by the spirit of Christmas

Today is filled with light
Not of stars or Christmas decor
But those in the children's eyes
And in the hearts of those around us

The gifts we bring
Aren't just toys and trees
It is our love of our fellow man
Our joy and hope for others

Smiles brighten the sidewalks
We parade by waving
Another year, another Christmas
Where even the strongest soul melts with compassion

Saying Goodbye

I heard the news you were sick
I didn't want to see you
I had no desire to visit the hospital
To see you in a weakened state

You the strong center of the family
The strength for all of us
Now needed us to be strong for you
And I could not find the strength

I refused and fought with the family
I did not want to be at your side
I could not see you ill and feeble
You and I had many long walks together

As the days grew closer for our flight to leave
I gave in to the hollering and the bickering
Joined the rest and prepared to see you
To hold your hand and help you

It was difficult to see you sick
But not as difficult as it was for you to need help
Weak and frail you refused any assistance
From anyone in the family but me

From your hospital bed to your home
Things looked good for your recovery
But we all knew that it was a façade of medicine
And you still needed the help you refused

Day in day out we came to visit
Now glad I came to your side
Affirming how close I was to you
Even though 7,000 miles separated us

We chatted over our few visits together
What we had done and shared
Speaking of family and friends
You let me serve the coffee tea and cookies

Each day was more difficult to say goodbye
You could no longer see us to the door
Sitting quietly in your chair
Speaking your love and waving

You could no longer hug us
Or walk us to the hallway
You didn't wave from your balcony window
And could not see us as we left

The final day had come
Our flight would leave tomorrow
You could not be there when we left
You could not see us off on our trip

I had thought that seeing you ill was difficult
In comparison I was wrong
Saying goodbye was near impossible
Leaving your side was tearing me apart

After a short visit I cleaned what I could
As my father, mother and brother said farewell
I saw the hurt in everyone's eyes
As they all stopped for hugs and kisses

Exchanging their love and thoughts
Each saying they would see you again
All knowing it would not be
Now it was my turn

I could not hug you tight
Your hurt enough physically
And both of us emotionally
I had to leave for home

As I said I love you and kissed your cheek
And held you as tight as I dared
I fought back my tears as did you
We had to be strong for each other

As I walked down the hallway
I looked back one last time
As you brought forth the strength to stand
You walked us to the door

One last kiss, one last goodbye
We left you at the door as we walked down the stairs
Not seeing you in the window we drove off
No one spoke a single word

The silence only broken by a few sniffles
This may have been my most difficult day
Knowing I would never see you again
Knowing that this was our last time saying goodbye

I'll Miss You

I was at work when the call came
We had all expected it
I thought I was prepared for it
I heard my mother's voice and began to cry

She hadn't even spoken your name yet
But I knew it was about you
It was the tone in her voice
The sorrow in her slow precise speech

I spoke to my boss and said I was leaving
I had to catch a flight that evening
Another short trip to the homeland
To weep and morn with my family

A month before we had said our final goodbye
Knowing your time would come soon
Only thankful it had come quickly for you
You did not suffer for too long

You fought until the last
Not once accepting help from anyone
Never allowing yourself to show pain
Fighting fear for yourself and others

I knew you had asked for relief
Aware that the doctor had killed you with comfort
I was happy you went with dignity
Still able enough to show your strengths

I will rest now

Sitting silent watching television
Relaxing not bothering anyone
Children milling around the house
A nice night with family at home

Shooting pain, doctor comes
He medicates you and says you're fine
Short visit, doctor leaves
You Shoo the children to their homes

All is quiet, time for the news
Your wife is on the phone
"Get off the phone" you yell
"Come here quick!"

As she runs up the stairs
You leave her and us
Silent you fall
The doctor was wrong

My Brother

I couldn't be by your side
I couldn't come say goodbye

We didn't speak enough
We did when it was important

You knew I loved you
You and I never said it

I missed you when you left
I will see you again someday

Look down upon me and know
I miss you, I love you, Your brother

Superman

Once I flew
Like Superman
My son he laughed
While others ran

Towards me

I got up quick
Jumped on my bike
I left the class
Rode out of sight

Home I went

At home I sat
For several days
I felt such pain
So many ways

Off to urgent care

I broke some bones
Placed in a cast
Confined to bed
Some weeks to last

My son apologized

Like Superman
Flying through the air
He thought I looked
Without a care

I ruined my gloves

So lesson learned
Don't hide the pain
And another day
I'll ride again

And I laughed when he broke something

A Prayer for a Morning Ride

Oh God What a windy day
Please get me to work on time

God help me
I don't know if I can handle this

My God the wind is so strong
Please put my sidecar wheel back down

Oh Jesus I can't control this
Help me

Jesus Christ don't let me hit that tree

Holy Jesus don't let me die

Christ I'm glad this tree kept me out of the ravine

Dear God give me the strength to get help

Thank the Lord
I'm alive

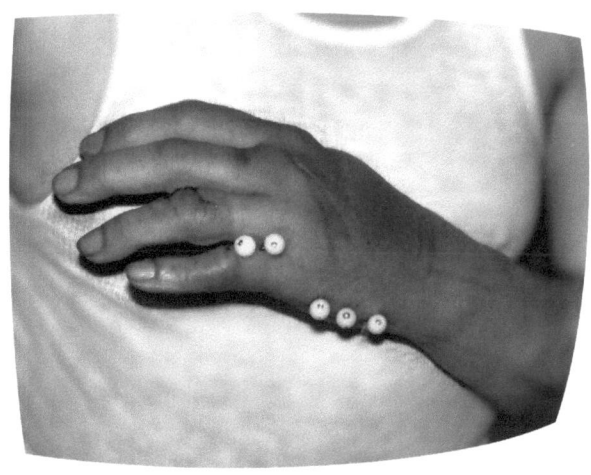

My Father Wore Tails

When I was young
I saw a photo
A beautiful young couple
The man wearing tails

I said to him
Wow that's neat
I want to wear them
As well someday

At his same age
I met my wife
And picked my tux
Because my father wore tails

My Little Girl

When my little girl was born
My father turned into a new man

He became the dad I always wanted
And the dad I wanted to be

He never rode bikes with us
Or played in the yard
Or let us touch his things

But then my little girl changed all that

I never knew what I missed
Until my little girl was born

Visions

I awake to what my future holds
Lush green meadows under alabaster skies

The contrast to the vivid memories
The nightmares of my childhood

Tears of joy and happiness
Mixed with the fear of my past

Happy with my family by my side
Knowing I will be alright with them here

My Family

Speaking for me when I can't
I understand everything around me
My body is broken but my mind is sharp
Lucid except for the nightmares

By my side every day
Knowing well I won't be around long
My family provides me strength
And I am strong for them in return

Providing me with all my needs
Never feeling like I am a burden
Happily waking, waiting, and helping
Allowing the final choice to be mine

My Son

My son he did for me
All of what a father does for a child

Held my hand when I was afraid
Gave me comfort when I was sad

He cared for me without asking
Came running when I needed help

We sat, we joked, we laughed
Silently sitting watching movies

My son I am so proud of him
Becoming the man I'd hoped he'd be

There are no good-byes,
Where ever you'll be,
You'll be in my heart.

~ Mohandas K. "Mahatma" Ghandi

Cold Kiss Goodbye

My mother called
Squeaking out "Please come home"
Riding home with lights and siren
That I don't have

Halfway home I slow
Knowing my speed won't help
And could make a bad end
Losing two wouldn't be good

Dashing into the house
I embrace my mother
We cry together for a moment
Then go in to visit my father

Staring at him in peaceful slumber
At rest from the pain at last
I reach over as I did every day we parted
And gave his forehead a final cold kiss goodbye

I hope to be like you someday

It took more Humility
For you to call for help when you fell
Than it took me to come help you up

It took more Resolve
For you to check into a hospital
Than it took me to come visit you

It took more Courage
For you to cry out in pain
Than it took me to hold your hand in comfort

It took more Strength
For you to get up and stand
Than it took for me to hold you up

It took more Faith
For you to let go
Than for me to let you

The pain I feel now is nothing
Compared to the pain you must have felt
Asking for help, being dependent
Not wanting to let us down

I miss you every day
I hope to be like you someday

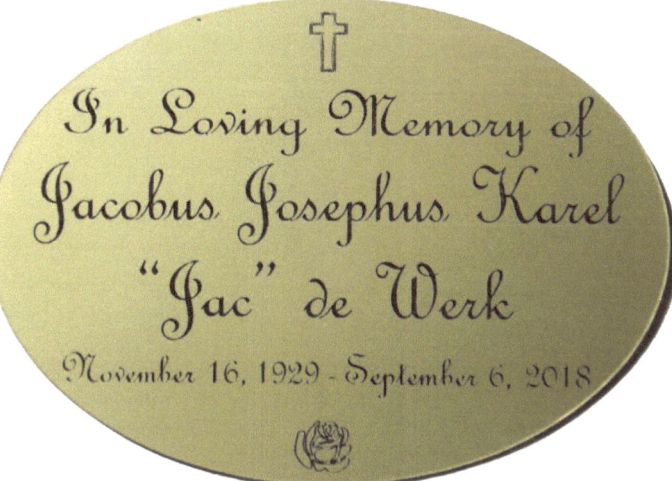

In Loving Memory of
Jacobus Josephus Karel
"Jac" de Werk
November 16, 1929 - September 6, 2018

Kind Words,
Open Ears,
Soft Shoulder,
Shedding Tears

I appear as extroverted
When shutting out the world
A façade of happiness
My mind tearing apart

I appreciate my friends
Who offer their Kind Words
And deeply cherish those
With the gift of Open Ears

A year today the passing
My father heavy on my mind
You friends so dear to me
Brings warmth into my heart

I will always remember
Your willing Soft Shoulder
Present without judgment
Allowed my Shedding Tears

The Poet

He is a knight
Or even a king
Alone in a castle
Walls of granite
Surrounded by a moat
Unable to lower his drawbridge
Or raise the entry gate
Alone he sits
Pen in hand he writes
Breaking apart the walls
Stone by stone they disappear
Until nothing is left but him
Open for all to see
For all to hear
The mighty pen has taken away his solitude
But also his protective structure
His feelings are in an open field
To be judged by no one
By everyone
This knight
This king
He is me
The poet

Image Index / Appendix:

Images:
Opposite page 1 - Photographer unknown, Public domain image of The St. Lawrence church in Rotterdam's city center after the bombing on 14 May 1940.
Only a few buildings survived the bombings. The most well known of these buildings is the Witte Huis, which was built in 1898 as the first high-rise building in Europe. Total destruction:
- 24,978 homes
- 2,320 businesses
- 24 churches
- 62 schools
- 775 warehouses
- 85,000 residence made homeless

Pg2: Photographer unknown, Public domain image of Rotterdam
Pg3: Photograph of "Verwoeste Stad" from Zadkine in Rotterdam

All photographs taken by Patrick A. de Werk the de Werk Family members.

Pg4: Airplane wing of the plane taken when immigrating to the United States
Pg6: Anne Frank huis, building front door
Pg8: Sunrisers Business card; Sunrisers band (Jac de Werk on Piano)
Pg9: de Werk family band; Jac on piano, Patrick on banjo, Paul-Joseph on drums
Pg10: 1972 Ford LTD station wagon crashed by Patrick (me)
Pg12: Mama en Papa (My mom and Dad Maritha and Jac)
Pg14: Jac riding on the back of Patrick's 1983 Goldwing.
Pg14: GWRRA chapter CA2J members gathering before an adopt-a-family ride during Christmas
Pg15: GWRRA chapter CA2J members gathering delivering Christmas
Pg18: First picture (l-r) Jac de Werk, Patrick de Werk, (Tante) Jeanette Korzilius (Jac's Aunt), Paul-Joseph de Werk
Pg18: Center left, (Tante) Jeanette Korzilius and nephew Jacobus (Jac). The rest of Tante Jeanette
Pg19: Bottom center, Tante Jeanette in Tracy, CA with Paul-Joseph (R) and Patrick (L).
Pg20: Karel de Werk (Brother of Jacobus)
Pg21: Brothers Jacobus and Karel de Werk (at the Grand Canyon)
Pg22: Jac on his Kawasaki KZ440. Gloves after his crash
Pg22: Patched up after his crash (l-r) Jac, Maritha, me, Cody, and Paul-Joseph de Werk
Pg24: Before and after pictures of Jacobus' vintage Goldwing after his morning ride crash
Pg25: Jac's hand after extensive surgery (8 hours to face and hand)
Pg26: Jacobus de Werk and Maria (Mann) de Werk on their wedding day
Pg27: Patrick de Werk and Kathy (Collins) de Werk on their wedding day
Pg27: My Father (Jac) on his wedding day.
Pg28: Pictures of Jacobus and Caitlin (his Granddaughter) (w/Patrick her Papa)
Pg29: Caitlin and her Opa (Grandfather)
Pg31: Me and my Father (Patrick and Jacobus)
Pg32: Kinderdijk, Nederland
Pg33: My Father's Urn at the funeral
Pg34: My Father (taken at a family celebration)
Pg35: "In Loving Memory" plaque on the wall at my Father's home
Pg36: Top left, Patrick de Werk and Carrisa Harrild; Top right, Vanessa Armstrong (used with permission from Vanessa); Bottom right, Katie Smith
Pg38: Me, taken in Lake Tahoe, CA

About the Author image taken by creative photographer Caitlin E. de Werk (CdeW Artistry)

About the Author

Patrick A. de Werk was born in Berkeley CA, to Dutch immigrants, a year after they came to the United States. Growing up he spoke both Dutch and English and was very fluent in both.

Patrick has traveled back to The Netherlands, with and without his parents, often. On one trip with his father, they shared an experience at the Anna Franke house, which was the inspiration for the well-received "Visiting Anne."

Being from musical parents he picked up Bluegrass Banjo at the age of 5, and played drums in several school and civic marching bands. Often playing with his father at the piano and brother at the drums. His father, had written several musical pieces, which were played on the radio by well-known bands of the time. Patrick took after his father and began writing himself. He wrote some music, but his early attempt at lyrics morphed into writing poetry.

Patrick grew up very shy, but expressive, having ADHD all his life, he found writing lyrics, drawing, and writing poetry, was a good way to express himself. Later turning to writing as a means to cope with experiences in his life. Which in turn helped his father open up when he wrote about parts of his father's life, that he wouldn't openly speak about.

With his passion for finding beauty and joy in all things, he writes about people, places, thoughts, and emotions. And while some of these may be sad, they are often good memories or experiences shared with others.

Patrick was ultimately challenged by his best friend C.J. to read in public. His writings were well received by the poetry community, opening him to further writing, and sharing at weekly poetry readings. He enjoys sharing his poetry with the people he writes about and for. With continued positive feedback he looks forward to the relationship with his words and the people that are moved by them.

What readers thought...

"The poem I liked the best, was the one about your dad dying.
I have stage 4 cervical cancer and was told they could not save my life. I dropped 50lbs in less than 3mos., I had 6 blood transfusions and was in the hospital for a week before I escaped.
I chose an alternative form of treatment with a low dose of chemo and immunotherapy infusions. My blood work is now amazing and they believe I will be disease free in just a couple months. I had a rough two years but here I am, gaining weight and getting stronger. I don't like being skinny!!
I had seen the fear in my children's eyes and that poem kept coming back to me. That made me fight hard. Without that desire to fight I would not have made it.
That poem saved my life."
  ~Lisa D.

"I must say this is very well thought out book of the life through his father's eyes. I felt every emotion while reading. And I thank you for letting the world feel your pain and your love and your reflections."
  ~ Vanessa A.

" To those who hold loving memories of a dear one in your heart, the books author voices his "Memories and Love for his father". He captures his father's life during WW II, love for music, adversity in life, as well as, his resilience to be the best family man to his beloved family...he is missed today with many loving memories."
  ~Vickie

"I also grew up during World War 2 in the Netherlands.
It is said that people that have not experienced war, do not understand it.
Patrick's words prove that he is both empathetic and understanding.
It helps me to read his words and to know that others understand."
  ~Ida R.

"You have a talent for writing. Your dad is looking down very proud of you."
  ~Katie S.

www.ingramcontent.com/pod-product-compliance
Lightning Source LLC
Chambersburg PA
CBHW052304200426
43209CB00061B/1719